ANCHOR BOOKS

PURE EMOTION

Edited by

Kelly Deacon

P.83 "The Scarecrow"

First published in Great Britain in 2000 by
ANCHOR BOOKS
Remus House,
Coltsfoot Drive,
Woodston,
Peterborough, PE2 9JX
Telephone (01733) 898102

HB ISBN 1 85930 830 9
SB ISBN 1 85930 835 X

FOREWORD

We are all individuals with our own thoughts, hopes and dreams, many agree that it is our personality which makes us the individuals we are.

In this carefully selected anthology new and established writers, men and women alike unite to share their thoughts about a number of issues.

The variety of subjet and sincerity of the poet makes *Pure Emotion* a favorite with all for many years to come.

Kelly Deacon
Editor

CONTENTS

ANONYMOUS

Her hundred year old eyes, bereft of hope,
show womanhood has stifled teenage spark.
No job, no man; however could she cope?
Her mental scars will leave no outward mark.
The kindly needle-sting escorts the dark.
Deep in this dark, my warm red cloak of womb
is torn from me. So bright, so cold! My doom
means all I might have been is but a dream.
Un-named, unknown, no requiem, no tomb,
and no one hears my terminated scream.

J Bates

EARTH WAKES . . .

Earth wakes
from the sleep of night
as the dawn sunlight
extinguishes
with living radiance
the glittering starfires
which lace the black fabric
of the sombre night . . .

At daybreak the kestrel
balances the wind
wings spread crucified
upon the cold hard morning air . . .

The bird is alone
in the empty sky of dawn
as the Earth spins
upon its invisible axis
while the human race
wakes sticky-eyed
to grumbling life
and harsh encounters
of the stress-filled
business of the working day . . .

But even now
mankind is reluctant
to shed the dream skin
of the snake of night . . .

Stephen Gyles

TIDES

The moon
drags her net
of silver
over the earth
and the spellbound seas
caught in the trawl
drift to and fro
in a celestial rhythm.

So too the rise and fall
in regular harmony
of the breath of life,
and the seasonal swing
of living and dying,
all in a wondrous
global orchestration.

Flood tides
of grief and passion
blindly rush
on a strong current,
pebbles lashed in turmoil
and seaspray biting,
enveloping, overwhelming, drowning.

Then the gradual ebb,
depositing, reshaping,
till all is calm again,
yet never the same
as the sandcastles of man
are always
washed
away.

Helen Dalgleish

SOBRIETY

My heart is
Handled in the close
Fibres of sobriety,
Like a leaf
Dropping, dropping,
Or blowing, blowing
Along the wind's
Soundless, swaying breath,
That which breathes
Like a warning awakening
Along my body
My own broad, scarcely bright body
And its movements are still silent,
And its
Funny head is not thinking;
Its laughter is close held
Like a small quiver on a flowing river.

Juliet Fowler

THE SHOOT

The guns, the beaters, and loaders,
   All ready for the shoot,
The dogs alert and waiting
   To follow in pursuit.

They really were a picture,
   Dressed in their country tweeds,
Some with their ladies beside them
   To see to their needs.

Of course the lord of the manor was there,
   But he only shot a hare,
Others shot well, their aim was good,
   And several braces fell in the wood.

At the end of the day
   Back home to dinner,
And talk of the day's sport,
   Soon they hope to enjoy
The birds they shot or caught.

I Millington

CAN WE HAVE A DOG MUM?

Can we have a dog Mum,
Please say yes.
We'll play with him and feed him,
Even clean his mess!
We'll get up in the night Mum
Should he start to bark,
And also in the morning
We'll be up with the lark!
He'll have lots of fun Mum,
Even lots more love.
He won't wreck the house
Or chew your favourite glove.
Please say we can Mum,
Some aren't much to buy.
You said you'd think about it
That means, 'Pigs might fly!'

Becky Garbett (13)

THE SWANS

With heads erect up to the sky,
the royal swans go gliding by.

Their silhouette, a fairy tale
casting shadows across the dale.

Lovers always, they remain,
linked through life with a golden chain.

He'll defend his love nie unto death,
and she'll love him with her dying breath.

So is the legend really true?
And could these swans be me and you?

T N McCarroll

THE OLD BROWN TEAPOT

Standing in a Flanders trench, the young soldier
Peered into the gloom, as he waited for stand down,
Which would signal the dawn, and rest from duty.
His mind turned to thoughts of home.

Sounds of shells, gunfire, war,
Blotted out by warm caressing visions,
Of a cosy kitchen, glowing in lamp light.
His mother busy preparing tea,
The old brown teapot warming on the hob.

His thoughts turned to dreams,
And he fell asleep at his post
To be awakened by shaking and shouting,
The sergeant and officer demanding explanations.
Inevitably the court martial followed.

The verdict as expected 'Guilty'
Punishment death by firing squad.
They pinned a white patch on his chest,
Tied him to a chair, then read aloud the charge,
He did not hear it, his mind was fixed on the old brown teapot.

In the little cottage, the fire had gone out,
His mother paused, shivered as she rekindled the fire.
In the bright flame she saw her son's face,
She picked up the teapot, the face disappeared,
Suddenly she knew, the teapot fell from her grasp.
She sank to the floor to pick up the pieces.

For sixteen years she had treasured them both.
Now they were gone, lost to her forever.

A R Lewis

EVERLASTING DANCE

In a beautiful dress with trimmings of white,
A vision of tenderness, my heart to delight
As she danced o'er the floor beneath the light's golden beams,
A vision that's seen, seen only in dreams.

I stood there just staring at that vision so rare,
Could she be an angel I saw dancing there?
Had she come down from heaven to dance at my feet?
If I ventured too near would that vision retreat?

Whirling and twirling to the melody's beat,
Weaving neat patterns with those small, graceful feet:
My heart beating faster, just longing to say
'Come to my arms to rest and to stay:'
Come my sweet angel, please don't drift away.

And then, by some magic, that vision of charms
I was holding so close, so close in my arms.
We were drifting and gliding o'er that heavenly floor;
'Dear God,' was my prayer 'let us dance evermore.'

A Woolley

THE BRUMMIE BOYS' HOLIDAY

Homely farm 'digs', the advertisement read,
'With modern amenities, breakfast and bed,
Plus evening meal and secluded quiet beach,
Also bus route and pub within easy reach.'

Well! The beach was secluded, that was quite true
Down a precipitous cliff for an odd mile or two,
And the bus stop though near didn't once mention that
The things only ran twice on 'Tues', 'Thurs' and 'Sat'.

With boiled cabbage and mutton each night we wrestled
Then retired to our beds, cold, lumpy and trestled,
We found the 'mod cons' searching anxious and hard
Were a pump and earth closet, across the back yard.

The 'pub' that was 'only a stone's throw away'
Proved to be six miles healthy exercise twice every day
Where we sat wet and unwelcome as the Welsh rain poured down,
Under watchful Welsh eyes, and suspicious Welsh frown.

One night we walked miles to go to a dance,
But all the Blodwens rejected the slightest advance,
And though after a week no one wished to stay longer,
We had to admit we felt fit, and our legs were much stronger.

E A Groves

MY LOVE

I love thee dear with all my heart
And will do so till death us do part.
I love thee like the flowers in spring
And have done since I wore your ring.
I love thee like the sun that shines above
As day by day we share our love.
I love thee like the gentle rain
Sharing our happiness and pain.
I love thee like the clouds in the sky
You can make me laugh and sometimes cry.
I love thee for all the things you do
And the wonderful times I spend with you.
I love thee as the darkest night
When a thunderstorm rolls and you hold me tight.
I love thee for the children you have given me
Paul, Helen and Mark make up our family.
I love thee for always being there when I needed you
But most of all I love you - for being you.
I love thee for the rest of my life
Thank you for choosing me for your wife.

Marjorie Ridley

A PASSIONATE HOPE

Good
and evil, black inscribed on
white
but white cannot be obliterated. Pages
of dense night cannot engulf when
light
has come. Fragmented
light
creates rainbows in droplets as they jump over rocks
true colours
fill the new page of day.
Live in light and love
permanently available, but ineffective until invited,
or in the dark confusion of
night, groping around for meaning. Switch on
love
turn over, and live in the unspoilt page of
light
and may each morning's new page
light up the darkness
of the world with
love.

Wendy Dedicott

THREE MINUTES

Come with me to a special place,
where grains of sand drift in space.
Drifting shadows within a spire of glass,
a ghostly desert with three minutes to pass.

Imagine streets of buildings old,
a ghost town of shops and houses sold.
Pass a stable of empty straw,
an old rusty carriage by a listing door.

Two minutes.

A peacock spreads his tail of eyes,
a proud display with breathtaking sighs.
A spectrum of colour from a narrowing neck,
spiralling waves on a sandy trek.

One minute.

Float with me through the tunnel of time,
sail on down with a gravity that's mine.
Braking now we're slowing fast,
leave this place your time has past.

John Hewins

PARADE OF THE GIANTS

The black stormy winter night
Outlines the parade of the 'Tree Giants'
They look like spectres with branches
Waving - limbs outstretched - fingers
Pointing accusingly and in protest.
Bark oozing, trunks splitting bare -
Their very souls uprooting, thrashing
About in despair. Finally, in twisted
Agony, they fall to the leafy ground -
The giants - spectres of the night
Finally at rest.

P I Bradford

SPOOKY

On natural lakes
I paddle my canoe
During the evening hours
Loons, hoot to one another
Across the vastness
Trees wave
In gentle breeze
All is at peace
Fish dip and dive, being nosy
Mystical sounds
Send shivers up and down my spine.

J M Stoles

THE A30 (LONDON TO LAND'S END)

If you want to go a-travelling towards the great south-west,
Then take the old A30, that's the way you'll find the best.
It winds from out of London and continues to Land's End;
It'll get you there eventually, on that you can depend.

Forget about the new M3, forget the old M4,
By taking the A30 you're sure to see much more;
You'll pass through Staines and Egham, at Camberley take a look,
Soon you'll reach Hartley Wintney, then it isn't far to Hook.

If you're from the south lands and you're one of the Hampshire's folk
You can't miss out a stop over in thriving Basingstoke.
Stockbridge is a pretty town and Salisbury is a city;
If you haven't time to look around then that would be a pity.

Through Wilton into Shaftesbury just across the Dorset line
While within that county a stop at Sherbourne would be fine.
You're heading on to Yeovil, to find it won't be hard,
Then carry on to Crewkerne and eight more miles to Chard.

When passing through these country towns the traffic's a disaster,
If you want to go to Honiton the three-o-three is faster,
But going further to the west you come to Exeter City;
Okehampton is another town the visitor finds pretty.

Then finally to Cornwall and Launceston comes before
You have to cross the lonely bleak expanse of Bodmin Moor,
Then Bodmin town and Indian Queen, the end's near, that's the truth,
Just twenty-seven miles to go once you've reached Redruth.

Then Connor Down and Hayle will lead you to Penzance,
If you want to stop before Land's End this is your final chance.
And so into the last ten miles; when you've arrived you'll know,
You'll have to turn and come right back - there's nowhere else to go.

Geoff Tullett

UNTITLED

Look inside.
A shambling giant of a man
Stooped down and stroked the baby's hand.
The infant gurgled, not upset
By nature's cruel disfigurement.
The infant smiled and chuckled on
But people stared and frowned upon
This shambling giant of a man
The beauty was inside this frame
But only one could see it
What a shame.
The baby stretched both arms out wide
A single tear from the man who cried.
The baby felt the sorrow grow
From where it came he did not know.
The innocent had touched the life
Of someone trapped.
The baby had felt the beauty near
But the spell was broken by a single tear.

Carole Walters

THE LADYBIRD

It's really getting quite absurd!
I'm followed by this ladybird.
At first it landed on my arm
And keen it should not come to harm,
I let it walk about my shoulder.
Consequently it grew bolder.
Crawling up my neck, I fear
It disappeared into my ear.
I tipped my head up on one side
But it was planning on a ride
Inside this tunnel, soft and dark,
She must have thought it quite a lark,
Until she stumbled on the drum,
An aural road sign, *Do not come.*
I heard a tiny voice inside me
'Please send help at once to guide me'
Thinking fast I found a tape
Of music that would make you gape,
It sparkled, sizzled, out of sight!
She stumbled out into the light
A little sticky, none the worse
For entering my universe.
And now this spotted creature goes
About the garden, tapping toes
And longing once again to hear
The jazz we shared inside my ear.

Ann Elliott Wall

BOYHOOD DREAMS OR SHADOWS OF THE PAST

I close my eyes, and drift away,
And think of years gone by,
How all the hopes and dreams I had,
All vanished in the sky.

I dreamt I'd be a pirate,
And I'd sail the seven seas,
I'd hold the crown, to ransom,
Wouldn't listen to their pleas.

I dreamt I'd be a soldier,
Seeking fortune, seeking fame,
I'd fight for king and country,
And have medals to my name.

I dreamt I'd be a cowboy,
And I'd ride a horse so white,
I'd conquer all injustice,
Fight the wrong and make it right.

I dreamt I'd be a doctor,
Treat the world for all its ills,
I'd find a cure for everything,
And there'd be no need for pills.

I dreamt I'd be a lawyer,
Fight for justice, fight for good,
Stop the crime, and all the killing,
Purge each town and neighbourhood.

These are dreams I had in boyhood,
These are dreams that didn't last,
They are memories of yesteryear,
Just shadows of the past.

F W Cumbes

PLOUGHSHARE

Plough and churn the open field
Which curves and hugs the sea-framed hill,
Fertile troughs to swell a new yield,
The turned fresh soil pursued by gulls.

Every open space is worked,
Farmyard machines occupy the lanes,
Sown and wrapped in a couple of weeks,
The early crop farmer's gain.

Ready to grow in cellophane,
Cloche effect for the warmer climate,
Until next year the ploughman wanes,
Crops are ripe for a summer fête -

Witness a rare treat and experience
The ploughman and his horse at work.

A J Lagadu

DREADED SPRAY

Spray! Polish me then buff to a sheen
Making our furniture all of a gleam.

Spray! Onto garden flowers and veg we put
Seldom using old fashioned soot.

Spray! I'm a substance that will kill every weed
For me you'll find a lot of need.

Spray! Onto all fields around
Soaking in to farming ground.

Spray! Yes it's me, here I come again
I'm the dreaded thing made by men.

Spray! I don't think I should ever been made
Perhaps it's why certain wildlife does fade.

Spray! Oh please don't use me anymore
Far better to have weeds and wildlife by the score.

J Cook

WHAT HAS THE WIND TO SAY TODAY?

What has the wind to say today
As through the trees it gently sighs?
Capricious and fickle in its play,
What maxims breathed profound and wise
In respiration to listening ears devise.

The restless trees in animated tones converse
In whispered words encouraged by the breeze.
Hear the gentle zephyr seeking to coerce
The leafy boughs to make music with enchanting ease,
Like an aeolian harp, delightfully to please.

Scent the wind persuading the blossomed hawthorn
To perfume the swaying, grassy sward.
Fragrant laden gusts are upward softly borne,
Presenting a piquant nosegay, sweetly adored;
The blessed joys of nature, generously outpoured.

View the sturdy oak upon a rise
With spreading branches murmuring in fervent prayer
In homage to the persistent wind that sighs
And penetrates each burdened, leafy layer;
Charming the casual viewer or curious surveyor.

See the foliaged hedgerow swaying in the blast;
The last resort of dispossessed and vagrant wildlife
From felled woodland and spinney of the recent past
And ploughed heath and pastured meadow alike;
Perpetrated by unthinking man, but causing nature strife.

Watch the wild parsley and redolent meadow flower
Cross swords with each other as the breezes blow;
While nervous furry animals in the thicket cower,
Awaiting vapour-laden winds to moderate and slow
And over hallowed nature a peaceful calm bestow.

Bryan Colman Bird

PASSIVE PEASANT

A down-trodden peasant in a pantomime,
right at the back, hidden I stand.
Front line would-be stars strut and prance,
sing lustfully out of tune to noisy band.

Not for me, costume of slipper satin pink,
pretty frills of lace, buttons shining gold.
But black skirt, uneven, torn hem, pinned,
ragged blouse, faded blue, years old.

Handsome Jack bypass without a word
to seek princess and starts to flirt.
I'm invisible to everyone but old Bill
and he's a penniless real smelly serf.

Teenage dainty dancers pose, fix smiled,
grim-faced ballerinas wobble on toes.
Arguments loud break out in the wings
between Prince Charming and producer, old foes.

Six foot dame, grotesque in flamboyant dress
over eye, starting to slip blonde golden wig.
Fluff funny lines and limping painfully
silver high shoe heel snapped in Irish jig.

Prompter, heavy cold, lose place in script,
panic, prince forget long important speech.
Overweight fairy burst tight flimsy bodice
while singing love song, ends in screech.

Saturday night, sparkling we give our all,
friends, relations, supportive gives hearty cheers.
Applaud, after bows/curtsy, curtain thud down
this passive peasant, in same place next year.

Phylis Smith

HEADLESS HECTOR THE NOISY SPECTRE

Hallowe'en! And I fear mad Sir Hector
Has been walking the west wing again,
For last night I heard moans and creaking of bones,
And the ominous rattling of chain.

He's turned up each year since they topped him.
At the spot where his victims were slaughtered.
It must be quite daunting to contemplate haunting
When once you've been hung, drawn and quartered.

But they must have refitted his entrails
For the task for which Hector was fated.
And one has to admit he's surprisingly fit,
For a man from his head separated.

The Victor prescribed exorcism,
As the way noisy ghosts could be grounded.
But the cleansing routine just made Hector more keen,
To judge by the way that he sounded.

I've tried guard dogs and man-traps and mothballs,
Made up balms for his aches and his pains,
I've renewed rusty locks and I've knitted him socks,
Bought some Castrol for oiling his chains.

Kept awake by his shrill lamentations,
I sought out the finest throat tonic,
And I hired a man from La Scala, Milan,
To make Hector's voice more harmonic.

But nothing, it seems, could deter him
From these spectral cacophonous jaunts.
So, I've just called to say that I'm going away
Till I hear it's close season for haunts.

Norman Ford

SPREAD YOUR WINGS

Like a secret
In your heart.
Feel the pressure
Of a broken heart.
There's no reason
To be alone.
Like a dream of love
Or passion zone -
Fly with me.

Spread your wings and fly away.
I'm not waiting for another day
To fall in love.

Like a secret
Deep inside.
Feel the pleasure
Of infanticide.
There's no reason
To be alone.
Like a seed of love
We've often grown.
Set me free.

Spread your wings and fly away.
I'm not waiting for another day
To fall in love.

Peter Steele

WITH PHILIP, TO ISRAEL

Like a shepherd you prepared us,
  Like sheep we followed you,
For without your love and guidance,
  We'd not known what to do.

We asked you questions and you must have thought,
  What kind of sheep are these?
Don't they know which is left or right
  Or their elbows from their knees?

From St Saviours to London Airport,
  Then our flight to Tel Aviv,
To have had a better guardian
  Is difficult to believe.

Onward we went together,
  To the sea of Galilee,
A view of peace and paradise,
  For all of us to see.

Then our walk by the River Jordan,
  When you helped us over the rocks,
When one old chap with a walking stick,
  Without help would have got wet socks!

Those heavenly days in Jerusalem
  That each of us spent with you,
Memories that will last forever
  And almost too good to be true.

And so Philip :-

We thank the Lord for having you
  As our shepherd and our guide
And know if trouble came to us,
  You'd be there - by our side.

C A Brush

MORAL DILEMMA - VIAGRA

When should they prescribe Viagra?
Should they treat everybody the same?
For pleasure, desire or something much higher?
Rekindling a dying flame?
Of course there's desire, and of course there is pleasure.
Recreating those moments we treasure.
Those moments, it seems, just go on forever.
When playing the sexual game.

The sexual game should be part of our lives,
If not then the word should be lust.
And if Viagra is used to this end, then where is the love and the trust?
For loving sex should be shared by two people.
Lifting them higher than the highest church steeple.
But if it's for one, then the reason is feeble
It's self satisfaction or bust.

But if you have love that has shared many years,
And where physical love is on hold.
The stress of your work, your family, your home.
On your health and well-being has told.
Then, yes! Viagra is for you and your wife.
To love one another. To enhance your shared life.
To calm all the years that were trouble and strife.
Enjoying each other, before you're too old.

There comes a time in each of our lives, when even Viagra won't do.
Those heights that we went to in earlier years, can never rekindle anew.
And as we remember the years long gone by,
We'll love one another, till the day that we die.
Sex? Well it lasted just a blink of an eye.
But our love will forever be true!

Tony Fuller

THE RIVER

Take me back to the river,
the sumptuous green river,
where time melts . . .
and days pass like gorgeous dreams.

I wish I were back by the river,
back in the time of the river,
when life was an adventure . . .
and death was a word.

Where mother nature lays down to rest . . .
in the warm glow of her own beauty,
and the garden of Eden, appears in a vision . . .
to the wide-eyed and unsuspecting boy!

Warren Tombs

QUEUES

Queues for compliant consumers
Desperately anticipating
A glimpse into the exotic
But finding only
The despotic
Grasping
Hand of profit
Behind every transaction.

Sue Johnston

BEER

A drink is good,
  a pint or two,
To lift the heart
  you raise a few;
But with the fourth
  an angel sighs,
And with your fifth
  all conscience dies;
At six the gents
  are heard to call,
Or else to pee
  against a wall;
The seventh one
  is just one more,
But still you fall
  upon the floor;
With eight you crawl
  back into bed,
And nine you'll
  certainly be dead.

David Matcham

YOU

Heisenberg was uncertain
I am not
I know that you are neither wave nor particle.
You are vapour.

You expand to fill the gaps in my soul.
You expel all doubt.
The hum of confusion is driven out,
Through valves in my ears I suppose,
Leaving behind your shimmering aura.

There is only one question . . .
It is outside the laws of physics.
How can someone, some presence, so pervading,
Wear such tiny shoes?

S N W Cross

MONDAY MORNING

The time of week I've come to dread,
Has once more dragged me from my bed,
And warily I brave the day,
To see what horrors come my way.

The Antichrist? The Third World War?
What lies beyond my bedroom door?
A minefield, maybe, on the stairs?
A bear trap in my favourite chair?

This time of week, I realise,
Has picked me out to victimise,
The postman's always at his peak,
He bit my dog this time last week.

The milkman's always full of life,
Especially since he stole my wife,
I wonder if I'm going mad,
For surely life can't be this bad?

The time of week I've come to hate,
Is ready for me, lay in wait,
So warily I make my move,
And pray I'll live 'til after noon.

Mark Cobbold

WINTER NORTHWISE

Those beautiful deer on the hills at the first fall of snow,
For winter has arrived again for all we know,
Animals of all kinds and shape scurried around making nests,
Storing their food here and there before heavy snow rests,
The beautiful antlers of the stag, like a large crown,
Standing on that hill with wondrous beauty so profound,
Against a background of pure whiteness so wonderfully clean,
From the apex on down to the glens a lovely scene,
Each crevasse and cave a shelter for all the animals you could see,
Preparing so hard for their winter quarters believe me,
Hares, rabbits and others among the ferns in the glen, trying to win,
Getting their food before the awful snow sets in,
Those wonderful large eagles out there on the wing,
Such wondrous beauty even in winter nature can bring,
The snow at present falls slowly like confetti to the ground,
Seems as if a wedding was about over with flakes all around,
Like some white garden of Eden the glens did seem,
A sea of white beauty, like some heavenly scene,
But! Soon the bitterness of winter will come to the fore,
Hiding all those animals, bringing the hard snow for sure,
Yet! The scenes of nature's wonderment will show its full light,
In different shapes of ice and snow beauty, a delight.

John S Johns

A CHILD IS BORN

You touch my soul
Gazing with intent
Nowhere to hide
Naked yet free
Of all illusion
I am seen
Eyes of innocence
A child is born.

Nicola Belle

EAST END HOPE

News that will only destroy,
Love's too frail to withstand,
Passing by the glass of time,
Fragments no more than sand.

Hope is the only window,
The chance that you were wrong,
He'll face the world a new man,
And fill your heart with song.

You know that cannot happen,
A dream and nothing more,
Pain that tore his heart apart,
Exposed the very core.

Lies and secrets held apart,
Make the distance great,
Secrets held away from him,
Could cause so much hate.

At last the time has come,
The truth now has spilled out,
Hope will spring eternal,
Only shadows of doubt.

On your own you'll stand tall,
Solitary, strong,
You, your child, no man,
Prove the world wrong.

The best chance for your child,
Not his anymore,
The right he lost, long ago,
The day he closed the door.

Goodbye Phil, when time has passed,
You'll realise what you've lost.

Philippa Larcombe

A COUNTRY LANE

Down this lane
I could dwell for hours
It's filled with tall trees
And wild flowers.
This wonder is Heaven sent
Close your eyes, dream,
Just breathe and smell the scent.
If this world is our earthly home
Think of the lanes in heaven
Where we will roam.
Can it be more wonderful than this?
Then I know that Heaven will be bliss.

Shirley Rowland

ENJOY YOUR CHILDREN

Enjoy your children while you may,
Treasure every childhood day,
Too soon your home they will have flown
As into adults they have grown.

Enjoy your children while you may,
Remember funny things they say,
So quickly computer speak to others
Usurps baby talk with mothers.

Enjoy your children while you may,
Share the things they do and play,
For some day they will share their life
With a husband or a wife.

Enjoy your children while you may,
But, be prepared to share one day
Your love - with their chosen spouse
And make them welcome in your house.

Enjoy your children while you may
Now, my sons *must* live and work away
I think of them across the miles -
Long to see their familiar smiles.

Joy Mullins

THE LUCKY CAT

The cat sat on the mat.
What a lucky cat to have a mat.
It could have been a cold hard floor
On which he set his weary paw.
What a lucky cat!

The cat sat on the mat.
And was that mat made all of wool,
Or was it made from luxury silk
Imported from a foreign shore
On which to rest his furry paw.
What a lucky cat!

The cat sat on the mat.
And did he catch his own juicy rat
Or was he fed on a china plate,
From a nice clean tin with a sell-by-date.
What a lucky cat!

I think I'll join that cat
And practice Yoga on his mat.
Perhaps he'll dream of a dish of cream,
And I will meditate and think of things,
Until yet again that darn phone rings.
And as I rush to answer its call,
The cat purrs on, oblivious to all.
And I think to myself, for the umpteenth time,
If I were a cat, I'd not answer that.
What a lucky cat!

Catherine Hartland

ALL I WANT IS THE SUN TO SHINE

All I want is the sun to shine and a friend to come with me.
We share it all, the walks and weather, the dog to guard us well.
The flowers are great, the colours and smell.
The green that never fails to come along our paths.
The birds sing well as we travel to new heights.
A view we find, old England's scenery nearer to heaven.

Rita Williams

IF . . .

If you could understand me,
If only you could see,
You'd realise I'm two people,
And I don't know which to be.

Beyond my outer image,
Lies a complicated mass,
A person of mixed feelings,
Who mustn't let youth pass.

Sometimes I feel I love you,
Sometimes I feel I care,
Yet other times, I do believe,
A mask of lies I wear.

I have no great ambitions,
I have no great desire,
I just need total freedom,
So my inner self won't tire.

If you could understand me,
If only you could see,
You'd realise I'm two people,
Who both need to be free.

Julie Belinda White

MORNING SUN

Smiling in the morning sun,
Shattered with the day begun.
Swallow tablets, try to breathe,
Outside the world, inside disease.

Cannot think, cannot move,
No one to comfort, no one to soothe.
Screaming, crying, to vent my rage
Locked inside my body's cage.

Just enough for me to be, tiny threads of sanity.
Static burns and blurs my head,
Trapped inside my once safe bed.
See the world through brand-new eyes,
Nothing here I recognise.

To dance inside the morning sun,
To feel, and think, and walk and run.
The ember of my essence lies,
Too deep to see, to cloak and hide.

Julia Bowler

AWAY FROM IT ALL

There is a place where I can be,
Away from all reality,
Away from all the trials of life,
From all the troubles and the strife,
Away from taxes, wars and crime,
From rape and drugs and fleeting time,
This place where I just want to be,
Are in my dreams, I shall be free,
And so the time has come for bed,
I pull the quilt right over my head,
Then drift into serenity,
Away from all reality.

John W Bendle

UNDER THE TREE

The clouds overhead, the rain starts to fall
As drop after drop spatters Love and me.
We take shelter under the giant oak
To wait to see if the shower will pass
So that we can make our way home.
We find we are all alone so Love clings
Closer and murmurs sweet words in my ear,
Words of love and deep devotion,
Words to warm the inners of my heart.
And so we kiss, a drop falls on
Our embracing lips to spice the already
Juicy flavour of Love's kiss.
And as the drops proceed, I hold her
Closer still until a rainbow breaks
The gloom. The shower stops, and Love
And I can proceed on our journey,
Whetted by the closeness of each other,
And warmed by the embrace
Of each other's love.

Thomas Splitt

BEGINNINGS

The seed is set, in the womb of earth.
It settles there to begin its birth.
First stirrings, ready, to put down roots.
Waiting - preparing - for those first shoots.
It's dark around - first dank - now warm.
A precious time, to prepare its form.
No rush is made now, to push ahead.
It chooses to co-operate instead,
With unseen forces from far above.
With sun and rain, with light and love.
For time should not be rushed or stormed,
For time allows, protects, informs.
It creates our links with what is past,
Then streams ahead - but not too fast.
For what is missed can't be regained.
The seed knows this so it's not strained.
It wants its roots to grow down strong.
To assure its shoots aren't weak and long.
It's happy now, in the womb of the mother,
She'll guard and guide and protect like no other.
She knows of the needs for the beginnings of things,
Sings them songs, helps them to rise, to what new life brings.

Jean C Hatherley

UNTITLED

I feel like I'm living, when
Love is good, lust kicks in
Beauty swims by.
Sunshine warms me
Dawn grows in a corner of the sky to cover ice in blue flame
Cicadas wake me.
Horizons glow red at night.
Food happens, my shoes fit, Sam the dog barks
Waves break right, or left
Money gets paid: on time, in time. For my time
Gin 'n' tonic is cold, lemon just-so, bitter.
Underwear don't ride.
Trees sound like rain, grass sweet against my teeth
Old friends call.
Traffic flowing, lights all on green.
Courtesy given. Taken.
Mist over the ocean, yachts reflected, still. Herons fishing
Sweet latte and good company, brown beer and humour.
Music from all the centuries I've lived
Dancing like a mad thing
For the glory of it.
Baby gurgles, soft hands big as my finger
First words
From all the above
And *you.*

Neil Benbow

ANNOYING

When I met you - you annoyed me
So you went away completely
When you came back I adored you
So you kissed me then - so sweetly
When you held me you enthralled me
So you did it once again
When you loved me on that special night
You scored ten out of ten
Then I said I thought I loved you
And the rot set in quite fast
So you sat me down and told me
That you knew it couldn't last
The only way you'd love me
Was if I was just your friend
So we're back to the beginning
You've annoyed me now . . .
The end.

Annette Zacharkiw

SIXTY YEARS YOUNG

We were born in 1940, we're the magical age at last
but we don't really feel any different to how we did in the past.
We're just a wee bit slower and we dither occasionally
but we're looking ahead, as we've been told, the best is yet to be!
It's time to get our bus pass, cheap fares to travel by train,
half price at the cinema, so we can afford to go again.
Free prescriptions from the doc, ear and eye tests free
vitamin pills and Sanatogen will be musts for you and me.
Ovaltine and Horlicks from the age concern shops
and although we've greying hair and glasses we still like
                                            'Top of the Pops'!
So we're sixty now and happy, life is simply great
but please don't call us OAPs - we're just past our sell-by-date.

Yvonne Catling

WHO IS A CHRISTIAN?

Christians are people who lead a good life,
Who care for their families, their husband or wife.
They may not be churchgoers, only they would know why,
But that isn't for others to question or pry.

Christians will always help others in need.
They do it for love, not for gain or for greed.
They will console the bereaved and comfort the sick,
These are the things that make a good Christian tick.

If they don't go to church it does not mean they don't pray,
For prayers can be said anywhere and anytime of the day.
Christians don't ask reward for the good that they do.
They can also do wrong just like me and like you.

Christians forgive any harm done to them,
They neither bear malice or seek revenge.
The good things they do are often unseen and unknown,
Except by the Lord from his Heavenly throne.

Phyllis Ing

INDECISION

Like the light of a candle
My mood flickers to and fro
Carried by an invisible current
From one direction to another.
Sometimes the current is gentle and warm,
Sometimes a maelstrom turning day into night.
Will the candle be snuffed out
Or be allowed to burn?

Elizabeth Whiting

MY FIRST FINGER

I have two first fingers, one on my right hand, one on my left.
The right is the first of the two, being useful and deft.
So handy a digit, its value is rich,
It can scratch my head when I feel a strong itch,
It can hold a needle to make a neat stitch;
When held straight ahead it can point out the way,
With a menacing wave it exhorts to obey.
When the cat's on my lap it will gently stroke
But in angry mood it will painfully poke
And the force it exerts is far from a joke.
When pressed to my thumb it will give a good nip
And when silence I ask it is pressed to my lip.
I can dip it in jam and steal a free taste
But this must be done in secret, with haste.
When crooked at the joint it invitingly beckons
And used with its comrades it arithmetic reckons.
Surreptitiously licked I can use it for wiping
But most precious of all for my one finger typing.
Unlike its companions it's adorned with no ring
But what would I do without the dear thing?

Mabel Hall

WINTERTIME

Now the days are shorter
Wind whistling round my ears
All the flowers over
Winter drawing near

The summer has been beautiful
But everything must change
Autumn colour in the trees
Such a lovely range

Blackberries in the hedgerows
Hips and haws as well
Food in plenty for the birds
In the winter they foretell

Lots of frost and ice around
Cobwebs glistening in the trees
Just like fairyland it seems
Like snowflakes in the breeze

Now it's spring, a pretty time
With flowers oh so bright
Daffodils and primroses
Fills one with delight.

Winifred Shore

SEPTEMBER

September, veiled by pastel autumn hue,
The sky above still brilliantly blue;
The greens fading to languorous yellow,
Dead stubble glisten brown under the plough.

Wild geese float in the waters of the sky,
It's time to go, their mournful parting cry
Hits the earth hard, then bounces back to fly
Away with them, to distant lands to die.

The rays of sun still abundantly spill
And bathe an orchard high above the hill;
The trees bearing red apples, standing still,
No breeze drifting, the landscape at standstill.

Colours of autumn without any taint,
What artist could you ever emulate?
Only the one, the almighty and great,
Puts on and blots out this transient paint.

Arpad Sarmezey

THE ULTIMATE PRIZE

Pressured by stress, not a moment to spare,
Focused like moths to the light of a flare.
High-powered jobs to pay for our leisure;
Prestige and power our coveted treasure.

Personal upheaval as loyalties change
While those once so precious are slowly estranged.
Distracted by lust in our jobs and careers,
Too busy to notice as love disappears.

Jollied along by imaginary friends
Acquiring new standards that nothing transcends;
Swept on a tide of pleasure and gain
Unfazed by the signs as our batteries drain.

Onwards and upwards we aim for the top,
No close friends or family to urge us to stop,
No place for emotion, no room for self-doubt,
If it entered our psyche we couldn't back out.

But where do we stand if we don't make the grade,
Swallow our pride and retire to the shade?
Do we talk to those people we used to malign
When we couldn't be bothered and didn't have time?

Cut off from the family and people who care,
Alone in the castles we've built in the air.
No kindred spirit to welcome us home;
Just the ultimate prize; a life of our own!

J M Redfern-Hayes

DREAMING

I dream of being on a pair of skis in the Alps,
having progressed from the nursery slopes,
to be in control, weaving and dipping,
down to the bottom, without a whipping.

Oh I am so graceful, a sight to behold,
nonchalantly holding on to my poles,
as I glide past all the others so serene.
Of course, remember now, this is only a dream.

For if I am awake, I must tell you now,
for 'tis untrue for me to take a bow.
For 'tis a sport I have never been able to master,
before this fable, goes any faster.

I could not even as a child, balance on a skate,
my peer group, so clever, I did hate.
I tried very hard, to get the knack,
but only ended every time, flat on my back.

I finally became accustomed to the spectator stand,
watching my contemporaries glide around;
I would smile, and wave, without a sound,
feeling small, and insignificant, my feet firmly, upon the ground.

So 'tis only in my dreams, I am graceful, serene,
dancing on ice to Tchaikovsky's Swan Lake,
when I am the swan,
and not the drake.

Such a marvellous transition, to be a part of a team,
with a mission,
so faultless, secure in every manoeuvre;
oh that it be I who can only dream, dream, dream.

Helen Philips

THE COMING OF SPRING

With the earth's awakening in the first sweet breath of spring
Man's heart grows lighter as he sheds
The burdening sorrows of the winter's ills
And lifts his eyes to greet the blossoming hills.

The trees burst forth in green and dainty splendour
And flowers do a gay gavotte in breezes tender.
Release your spirits man and with the dancing trees,
Give thanks that spring is here, and winter now has passed another year.

Dewdrops like fairy necklaces sparkle on the lawn,
The birds are nesting in the trees waiting for the dawn
To sing in chorus sweet, loud and clear
Calling wake up, wake up for the spring is here.

Muriel Johnson

GREEN TO GREY

There once meandered a stream
Bursting banks teaming with wildlife
Overhanging vegetation
Dangling roots in cold clear water
Supping freshness under forested growth

Till the roots began cringing
And capillaries death to its stem
The water hastening to dilute
The chemical flow
Rays burning lushness away

Enduring the occasional
Sprinkling of acid drops
The motionless fish swim
Leaving a gangrenous wake
Floating into steel projections
That turn our pastures
From green to grey.

A Cartlidge

IN THE CLOUDS

You sprawl on your back on a warm cloudy day
watching white clouds as they drift by your way.
Half closing your eyes you lay in comfort and quiet,
letting your brain free-wheel, your imagination run riot.

The clouds will meander into the shapes that you think
as across your narrowed vision they so gently slink.
Some of the shapes will have beauty, others will not,
but they are all oh! so fleeting, gone in a jot.

As those fluffy clouds billow like a mountain up high,
your wandering mind will distort them, without having to try.
They will reflect that deep secret, that innermost thought,
and in one precise moment your hidden feeling is caught.

The soft edge of the clouds waft around here and there,
of their subtlest changes you are hardly aware.
They change the thought patterns at the back of your mind,
those cotton wool clouds begin to appear silver lined.

Your tired brain will slow down as you drift nearer to sleep,
those passing cloud images will become easier to keep.
They will last that bit longer, and become more defined,
forging a link in the sky between the clouds and mankind.

If your thoughts are in turmoil, both troubled and black,
the nightmarish sights formed will take you quite aback.
If you're at peace with yourself, both calm and serene,
those soft rounded clouds will form some heavenly dream.

It's a wonderful feeling to be at one with your cloud,
being devoid of all worries, your spirit unbowed.
Having had thoughts most profound on many subjects so deep
you yawn 'what does it matter', and nod quietly to sleep.

Martin V Ullathorne

SIREN

You can hear my voice calling; so sweetly, so pure.
You weep with the sound that fills your heart.
Come to me, my true love, join with me now.

Enchanted, you seek me, but come nearer still.
You'll love me and want me 'til madness takes hold.
I seduce you, bewitch you - you cannot resist.
Your destiny lies here, with me, my love.

You see my beauty - do I not please?
Come to me sweetheart, hear my song.
I am the embodiment of your innermost desires.
I charm you, I possess you; beguiled by my passion,
you're mesmerised,
your downfall is weakness, my dear.
Yield; you must yield. You can do nothing more
than surrender your life to your fate.

So easily tempted, you must pay for all men,
and all men will pay for you.

Come, join in my chant; you'll love me the more you submit.
Your torment is deserved, but I'll give you bliss.
Touch me, beloved, and I grant you your wish;
but your soul will be mine tonight.
Your frenzied mind will once more find rest,
so abandon yourself to my love.

You're close to me now, and you reach out to beg,
as the fire in my eyes strikes you dumb.
You realise your fate and the frailty you own.
Fall to your knees, my weak-willed deceiver,
and we shall be as one.

My true love - do you hear my song?
It will hypnotise your soul.
Come, sing my words and fall in love -
I'm the one whose heart you stole.

Johanna Williamson

DAYBREAK

The calm still sea just glistens
As the sun rises up above
And as I stand here watching
I think about our love.
The clouds form pretty patterns
As they float across the sky
And once again I think of you
And gently breathe a sigh.
The coastline's silhouetted
As the night breaks into day
And as I watch this movement
I want with you to lay.
It's now almost complete
As the sun comes shining through
And once again in beauty
I can only think of you.

Sue Yorke

SHEATON'S TOWER

Upon Plymouth Hoe, a lad stood bewildered
A lighthouse on dry land? How can that be?
He looked to his father, a pillar of knowledge
Who said to his son 'Well it's like this you see.'

Since 1696, out there in Plymouth Sound
The seamen have been guided, on their journeys homeward bound
Four lighthouses to date, on eddystone have stood
The last two cast of stone, the first two made of wood.

The first two wooden structures caught fire, burned away
Then Smeaton designed a tower of stone, the one you see today
A hundred years and more it stood, until the fateful day
The rocks on which the tower stood, began to wash away.

On firmer rock, an engineer called Douglas built another
Leaving Smeaton's derelict, the stormy waves to smother
The locals got together, bought the tower, pulled it down
Moved the blocks, one at a time, into old Plymouth town.

In 1882, it was rebuilt, just as it was before
So here it stands aloft again, this time upon the shore
A piece of local history, no longer casting light
Yet, still it catches people's eye, a quite outstanding sight.

David Strauss Steer

YOUR HOME

Early this morning,
I watched them
pack up and take away
all that was your home.

I decided not to keep
odd bits of furniture
your books or an old stick
that your brother once used.

I don't need the standard lamp
that once gave you light to read
in our first home, when I was small
and I played on the floor behind you.

I've no use for the brass bowl
you used for tapping ash
from cigarettes you stopped smoking
after reading about cancer.

Nor space for the travel clock
from mantleshelves
in homes where I grew and left
and returned again for your wisdom.

In the empty bedroom
why do I see you lying there
trying to understand how morphine
could ease, not extend your suffering?

Why do I care so much?
They are just things
in a house that is up for sale
but remind me of you.

David Firth

POLITENESS

What happened to please and thank you,
Have they become obsolete words?
For it seems to me that nowadays
They are very seldom heard.
When I was young I was taught to acknowledge
Every kindness and gift received,
And if I forgot then I was told,
That I was very bad mannered indeed.
What a pleasure it will be in the future
If we all remember those words,
And every time when they should be used
Please and thank you are once again heard.

Ivy Neville

FOLK SONG

I walk through fields of waving corn,
Away from where my baby lies dead;
Away from the home my son was just born in,
Away from my girl who's dead in my bed.

   The sky's on fire and so is my heart:
   The burning shame of what I have done:
   I couldn't love and see her depart, so
   I killed my girl and very own son.

Why did our love go ragged and torn?
Oh wind, please blow my sorrow away;
Listen waving ears of corn, so
Why did I do it? What can I say?

   The trees are dancing, feel my despair,
   Black against the angry sky.
   Nobody answers, no one is there,
   Just ears of corn, and they can't cry.

She screamed tonight our boy was not mine.
How could she hurt and torture me so.
I couldn't stand the jealously in me,
So I decided they'd have to go.

Shirley Arnold

MOUNTAIN MOMENTS

I will sing a song of the melting snow
Of the soft white blanket that cries away
Itself far down to the valley below
In cold streams of tears by sun's warming ray

How soft is the snowflake, how brightly white
It shines as it drifts in the gentle breeze
As soft as your cheek, as your smile so bright
Which beams at me at loving times like these

We sit entwined and watch the Alpine scene
Wrapped up closely against the winter chill
White snowy peak to dark green wooded dene
Melt into each other with ardent thrill

As melting snow passion passes away
Tears of joy shed in the sun's dying rays.

John M Spiers

THE GREY SQUIRREL

I saw it in the stark wickerwork
Of the gnarled old oak
Silhouetted against a doleful, grey sky.
The darting movement caught my eye
And there it was trapezing,
Daringly from branch to branch,
Its long arched tail following
Its small agile body.
A drier, milder day after
Yesterday's first fall of snow,
It had dared to leave the cosiness
Of its drey, never one for long hibernation!
Provisions must be low
After such a long, freezing winter!
But soon the proud mighty oak
Will provide more leafy protection
For its antics, while developing fruit
Ready for squirrel's autumn store.
In long summer months the little grey rascal
Will become more adventurous.
Its sudden leaps and bounds will bring
It onto the garden wall where
I will watch it crack a nut
Nimbly between finger-like paws,
Sat on its haunches, bushy tail
Curved gracefully against its back
And, oblivious to my total fascination,
Ravenously enjoy its repast.

Pat Heppel

LIFE CYCLES

Life is like a circle from the cradle to the grave
We are born into this wicked world, a tiny helpless babe
Our parents choose some names for us
We are christened and well blessed
Accepted into God's house - He will do the rest

As we go through childhood we learn so many things
An infant, then a toddler, and all that this stage brings
Then comes our teenage days, young adults now are we
There's still so much more to learn
And sights for us to see

If you are a lucky one and find a loving spouse
Marriage is the next step and looking for a house
We then have children of our own
If we are so blessed
The years pass by so quickly, not much time to rest

Suddenly you wake one day and then you realise
Retirement is nearly here, this comes as a surprise
Time to take life easily, no more rush and tear
Do just what you like and when
Time to stand and stare

As old age creeps onward and the years pass quicker still
If you are very fortunate you will be fit and well
The world has turned full circle, happy memories remain
So count your blessings every one
And joy you will retain.

Verity Denton

THANKSGIVING - OR LAMENT?

School holidays are over, I heave a grateful sigh,
no more early rising, I've waved my last goodbye:
No crackling crisps down the settee, broken biscuits on the floor,
no bikes parked in the kitchen, no banging on the door.
No quarrelling over who will carry cricket stumps or ball,
no tripping over trainers left halfway down the hall.
No fighting off the drowsiness that settles about three -
there's time to put my feet up and think of only me
and when it comes to lunch time I need only set for one;
it's very nice, it's peaceful - but it isn't half the fun!

Brenda Heath

FEBRUARY

Wet rubbish month. Discarded cans
In swollen, muddy streams
All rusty and forgotten,
The trees stripped bare
Awaiting spring
Like skinny dippers on the river bank.

Cars, like boats, spray their way along.
The promenades, deserted, stare
Eyeless at the sea.
And people wipe away the mist
From windows.

Horses, hedge-huddled in the mist
Face the low grey skies.
The rain, in rotted tree boles
Makes acid pools, and tumbled over
Straining weirs, the autumn's remnants fall.

But at moments of the rain's respite
The shaggy month looks up
And hears the music of the gutters
Sees spring beneath the mud
And know the reason why the hedges
All bejewelled, sing with scruffy birds.

Tim Williams

LIFE

To come deep from the comforting darkness
To a piercing ray of light
Is the tiny human with no say
In what is to become his plight.
His body-wrenching, writhing, wriggling -
Struggling to be free.
A fact that he'll soon realise
Just cannot ever be.

Nicola Westell

THE CROSSING

'Straight to the kerb,' I said to my friend
Now to the shops our way we must wend.
Just as I spoke, my arm was gripped tight
Pulled to one side, it gave me a fright.
Before I could speak we were crossing the street,
Cars fore and aft, my legs felt quite weak.
'I've got you across' said my arm-gripping man
Yes thanks, I thought to die was your plan.
'Where are we now?' I asked, pondering my fate,
There was no answer, my dog gave a shake.
'Can I help you?' said a small childish voice
'Oh yes, yes please. Butcher's shop is my choice.'
Then holding my hand, I was led along gently
To a pelican crossing, where the bleeps bleated softly
With care and attention I was led over smartly
My guide dog beside me, his head held up proudly.
Both of us grateful to the little Girl Brownie
For knowing the code on crossing the road safely.
Guide dogs are trained to help each blind owner
Cross the road safely and not get run over.
Kind persons, take heed when blind people you see,
Ask if help's wanted - look what happened to me!

Lillian Baxter

NOT A PRESENT . . .

The best thing I ever received
In the whole of my life
Was not in the form of a present
It had no bow or wrapping paper
No little tag with well thought verse
Neither did it arrive on an occasion
It wasn't even wholly for me

Like a pet it could be loved
Like a teddy it would be cuddled
Like a game it could be played with
Like money it gave independence and freedom

It was something I received
That would outshine everything else in my life
It would be respected and appreciated
More than anything I would ever know
The thing I received was a person

This person came into my life
Gave me a chance to grow
Surrounded by love, affection and security

To stand by me when others let me down
To listen whilst others walked away
To guide when my steps went off track
To love me for who I am

The best thing I ever received
In the whole of my life
Was not in the form of a present
It was in the form of the greatest person I know
That person was my dad.

L J Futcher

EVERY ONE A WINNER

At the debutante gathering with a nightingale choir,
Dahlias parade in their finest attire.
Hollyhocks saunter onto the floor,
Curtseying low to the rapturous roar,
From the hybrid lupins who sing out a song,
At this fashion parade, for the flowering throng.
Snowy white peonies prance to the front,
A dig of elbow, makes the pampas grass grunt.
Upper crust lilies look behind with a glare,
At the bearded iris who blatantly dare,
To make suggestive remarks about the strong lily scent,
Such a glorious balm, no offence was meant.
Silken poppies breeze in from the rear,
Their delicate beauty, brings a unanimous cheer.
On this particular day the pride of first place,
Is for viola bambini with a sweet elfin face.
Competitors call for the traditional speech,
The viola responds with a blush of the cheek.
Each flower is a star, the viola knows well,
An award is given to all those who dwell,
In this paradise garden, a haven to share,
For flora and fauna, to love and to care.
At the end of the day the nightingales sing,
Nature dreams, of what tomorrow may bring.

Jane Rennie

ANGLING IN DELIGHTFUL DEVONSHIRE

The virile whip of wind
Encouraging cheeks to freshness
And a stimulating glow,
Of exultation from a cheering, warming sun;
Or balm of breezes
Cooling on the brow:
That is why men and women
Go to fish.

An otter breasting water suddenly
Seems like a passing, personal friend.
Wild birds in chorus, singing eagerly,
Offering spontaneously the glories of a natural choir:
That is why men and women
Go to fish.

Bright, busy butterflies of vivid hue
Come fluttering, sporting up and down the banks:
Swift, airborne, colourful cameos
Of delicate delight:
That is why men and women
Go to fish.

Then -
When the evening comes,
With rooks in squadrons zooming home
Towards favoured trees and nests,
And cattle call in mournful camaraderie;
Come stealing soft white breaths of mists
To shield, protectively, the well- loved fields
Of dreamy Devonshire -
That is why men and women
Go to fish.

Richard Flemington

STANDING STONES

As great galleon clouds
Cruise the peak of Kes Tor,
We swam with the winds
Amid mire seas of high moor.

While their swift silent darkness
Sweeps the heather and grass,
Their running shadows urging us along
Rough, wet, uneven paths.

Yet, what deep secrets does this landscape hide,
This awesome empty place?
And in our inquisitive researching stride,
Chill winds do numb our face.

To where ritualistic piles of bones
Of Bronze Age hunter gatherer men
Were buried close these standing stones
In a Neolithic dolmen.

We marvel how their masons' skill
Has withstood the test of time.
And could the mysterious vastness of this ancient moor
Have been their deity divine?

But, whatever gods were worshipped here,
At this temple, by those people,
The great walls are immense, of open air,
And the surrounding tors the steeples.

So with sodden socks and aching feet
We rest and wonder at this timeless scene,
As against their sacred stones we make our seat,
Near the rising of the River Teign.

Eric J Last

SUNSET

At sunset time I like to be
High in my bedroom window
To see the birds, in twos and threes
Winging home, high in the pale silk sky

Pale now, but ever-changing -
Gold, then fiery red streaks across the horizon
Fade to rose, amber and cinnamon
As the sun sinks slowly in the west

Gone now, and the sky becomes
Turquoise silk with purple clouds
Then lavender and violet through to indigo
With the first bright stars filling the heavens

Diana Price

'HE GAVE ME SUN AND STARS AND AUGHT HE COULD BUT NOT A WOMAN'S LOVE . . . ' GKC

I was young, and I dreamed and believed in what seemed as a light
through life's tortuous ways,
Wherein love was the treasure in which lay the measure and value
of all our days;
I was sure in my youth of the positive truth, that every creature
on earth might
Sweet such sweet wonder, for each soul under the sun a certain
birthright.

For a time then I toyed in a tenuous void in peripheral pleasures
of passion,
And awaited the balm of a love, pure and calm of a steadfast,
unyielding fashion
Like a delicate plant, which would flourish enchanting in beauty
beyond all conceiving:
While time trembled on, and the green days were gone, I believed;
and I went on believing.

Now I am old, and touched with a cold like the depths of the
permafrost,
And the dreams which I knew, the delight of a few: For the rest
but a vision lost.
In the sunless grey of a waning day I remember my barren belief,
While the sap which rose in the spring now goes to earth
in a withered leaf.

One ephemeral season of flower beyond reason and hope
was my only fulfilment,
'Til the sweet fruit declined and was sadly consigned to the earth,
where my heart and my will went.
All my soul could invest in, a beautiful destiny, proved the
more bitter illusion:
A slow-dimming light of our hopes and our sight is life's only
predestined conclusion.

Paul de Mapingham

A PENNY FOR YOUR THOUGHTS

I've often wondered the value of money
If the best things in life are 'free'
I guess possessing something, encourages greed
But can you take it with you when you die?
Knowledge!
What price would you put on that?
A penny for your thoughts
These words I'm using are free to us all
Maybe I have a clearer mind,
But I don't think so!
I have money, but it's not mine
For it's only a means to purchase
I suppose I could charge you for reading this
But why should I
What do you think about?
I'd be happy to listen
We might learn from each other
Imagine that!

Carl Haggerty

MISSING HIM

Stirring in the dead of night,
Awakened by a dream a fright.
I reach for him but he's not there,
The bed was empty, no one there.
For a second I wonder where he's gone,
Then I realise what is wrong.
I start to cry,
It's all a dream,
I lay there thinking, I want to scream.
It's been four years since he passed away,
I miss him still, every minute, every day.
But he's at peace and free of pain,
I know one day we'll meet again.

S Raven

A PEACOCK FOR CHRISTMAS

Of all the Yuletide thoughts that linger,
Was a peacock feeding on my finger.

It's long thin proboscis slowly uncurled
As it stretched to explore this festive world.
A tickling sensation strange to describe -
That thread-like tube sucking up its food.
The wings seemed to flow with energy new
As around our Christmas tree it flew.

Flapping and fluttering, a colourful palette,
Dipping and diving, an aerial ballet -
Showing off its peacock hue
With wings no artist could construe.
Outstripping every decoration
A flaunting, preening elevation.
Purples and pinks and midnight blue,
Emerald, vermilion - around it flew.

I think it had a good Yuletide,
Had it been outside it would have died.

Of all the Yuletide thoughts that linger,
Was a peacock feeding on my finger.

D M Cudmore

GOD

He lounged on fluffy white clouds
The timelessly old, old man;
Whose shock of light hair and beard
Were not styled to any particular plan,
To her childish mind.

Sprawled in his marshmallow heaven,
Watching over her always,
She thought of him - a good God,
And loved Him so much and was full of praise
Of a face believed kind.

A small trusting girl he found then,
Who looked up to Paradise;
When, by a stray word or deed
Brought anger or tears to another's eyes,
She knew it was unkind.

Then, it was all so clear and bright,
Accepted in her child-like way.
A glowing haven up above
Where He reigned supreme, guiding come what may,
Like leading the blind.

The darkening clouds of conscience,
Now shadows thoughts of above -
Him - amongst His marshmallows,
Does she still believe He's there, full of love,
Is that what she'd find?

Susan Naile

CHILDHOOD MEMORIES

Sunny days of picnics in the park,
Tomato sandwiches, lemonade,
Heading home long before dark,
Tired, worn, grubby, but happy.

Holidays in caravans by the sea,
Donkey rides on sandy beaches,
Then back to the caravan for our tea,
Tired, worn, grubby, but happy.

Special treats to special places,
Travelling by train, is it diesel or steam?
Homeward bound, sleep in the sun,
Tired, worn, grubby, but happy.

Sunday school trips to the moors and back,
Where we go is no longer a 'mystery',
Views picturesque topped by ice-cream snack,
Back seat homeward, singing songs brightly,
Tired, worn, grubby but happy.

Special days with Mum and Dad,
Pantomime, picture shows,
Car and phone we never had,
School transport on bike behind Dad,
Home, tired, worn, clean but happy.

Lynda Burton

The Scarecrow

I see you, Scarecrow, standing here
Wearing your sartorial gear.
You're lost for any form of words,
Just posing here to scare the birds.

Your turnip face, ill-fitting shoes,
Baggy trousers, ragged blouse
All tell a story centuries long
About a scarecrow big and strong

Hands outstretched, legs never bending
Hat askew and gaze unending
Who tends the rows of fragile crops;
Whose concentration never stops.

For aeons now you've stood the test.
Of all bird scarers you're the best!
No reason why a thousand years
Should change your face or nose or ears.

So carry on my handsome fellow
Until crops turn from green to yellow
Scare the sparrow or the crow
Until the farmer comes to mow,

And then, equipped in summer's gear
You'll stand forlorn till end of year
When farmer Giles will bring you in
The new millennium to begin.

Dymoke Jowitt

BOBBY'S BEADS

People stood gazing upwards.
All of them wearing very dark glasses;
special ones for the occasion.
First it was Bobby's beads,
or was it Baily's beads?
Either way there were beads.
Then came the diamond ring.
A beautiful golden ring,
with a bright shining diamond.
It must have been the biggest diamond,
ever to be set in gold.
Totality.
Complete and utter darkness.
The air went icy cold.
A strange atmosphere for the middle of summer,
during the day,
darkness and freezing cold.
The diamond ring came back.
That beautiful golden ring,
entertaining the company of the diamond.
Bernie's beads, no Baily's beads came.
An amazing view to see;
and it's the last one of the 1900s.
It would have been such an amazing view,
if it hadn't been cloudy!

Jenny Masters (16)

THE MOUTH

Soft, beguiling
Infinitely tender
The mouth receives
Responds and would
Go on forever

The chemistry zings
The mind stands still
While sheer pleasure
Fills one's being

Slowly the tantalising tongue
Explores the yielding flesh
Then probes urgently
To indicate desire

The scent of Armani
Mingles with Chanel
Mixed with strawberries in summer
And champagne diurnally

A scratchy shave
Sends small tingles of shock
While a moustache
Can be surprisingly gentle

Nothing can compare with the mouth
The most intimate area of the body
With-held by prostitutes
But offered profusely to babies

The mouth has many functions
It eats, it talks, it shouts and smokes
It blows bubbles, raspberries
And musical instruments
No one should underestimate its worth

June Lander

PASSING BY

What years have I seen pass by
Since my youth of long ago!
What knowledge have I gained!
A true understanding -
Not fame neither shame -
We tread those same long
Lanes where little has changed.
Each season comes and goes.
Now even the birds seem less in number -
Or is it my on-coming habit to slumber -
While young life softly flutters by
Much too quick for my tiring eye?
Soon I must awake to see that shining light
Far above the sky so bright.
Each star has a welcome glitter -
Maybe I will see a shooting star -
Or better still it may be little old me?
We shall surely see!

Norma Pusey

LOVE LIGHT

Heavy rain clouds break asunder,
letting through a shaft of light.
Glances off a hanging raindrop,
changes it to jewel bright.

Gentle breezes move the branches.
Make the raindrop dance and sway.
Rainbow colours flash and glisten,
brightening my gloomy day.

Coloured lances wreak gay havoc
with the darkness of my room
as the miracle of colour
penetrates the deepest gloom.

Sparkling jewels all around me,
rainbow colours find their mark.
miracle of love surrounds me,
probing deeply to my heart.

Raymond Black

A MESSENGER IN TIME

I feel like a messenger between the past and the future,
Not able to let go of the past,
Not able to see into the future.
The ghosts of the early departed being a constant reminder
That the future actually contains the past.
All that we have known,
All those we have known
Are already where we are going.
There is nothing we can experience to compare with the
ultimate experience.
Our future is and must one day be the past.
This is the one thing no one and nothing can change.
Time being the great leveller.
The mighty and the minute, the mouse and the man will
eventually arrive at the same point in time.
The past!

T W Denis Constance

SOLDIER BOY

Heads bowed, trumpet played,
All forsaken in the sunken grave,
Prayers and hymns, delicate flowers,
To remember others, in happier hours.
War is over, peace at last,
Now they've carried out their task.
Our thoughts are with them, memories too,
Our flag is flying, red, white and blue.

Glennis Stokes

A Very Civil Servant

Bangers and mash on Mondays,
Tuesday that will be steak,
Bubble and squeak on Wednesday night,
Bubble and squeal I'd take.

Bubble and squeal
Bubble and squeal
Oh give me bubble and squeal!
Pencils sharp, rubber right,
Bubble and squeal be mine tonight.

Me on top, you below,
Must be Thursday,
That's the way it goes.

Remember when we used to kiss?
Your lips pressed next to mine,
Before you had your dentures,
And I had too much wine.

Remember our desire, as our clothes began to peel,
Please forgive me Dorothy,
I'm going to bubble and squeal.

Did I please you Dorothy?
Did you bubble and squeal?
Please get off now Dorothy,
Go and make my meal.

Ralph Collier

A Secret Place

Old Tom, of the 'Residential Home for Gentle Folk',
Was told that he was much more fortunate than most;
Just because of the fact that his designated chair
By the window, had a scenic view of the coast.

Though he mentioned that he held no regard for the sea,
But loved the countryside where he was born and bred -
Woods where the blackbird woke at dawn and owls flew at dusk,
But they just smiled, dismissing what the old man said.

So, Tom resigned himself to his chair by the window.
And because he had a benign look on his face -
They concluded that he was content there after all.
But his smile hid memories stored in his secret place.

Jean Stephens

A POET EXAMINES HIS RAW MATERIAL

See, admiration, love are merely words.
'Tis what they cause in minds and souls that matters
And nuances around them each one girds -
A different set for me and he who natters.
    Communication is a wondrous tool
    But he who thinks it is exact, a fool.

The problem differs word from word. That's clear.
A turnip is as plain as plain can be.
No chance of miscommunication here?
Do turnips have nuanceability?
    Just ask the farmer smiling in his field
    And then the girl who has to get them peeled.

With words like good and evil, afterlife,
Morality, nobility and such
Is where this wretched trouble is most rife.
A man speaks English - I hear double-Dutch.
    It would be rude of me to say he's daft,
    Matched only by his rudeness when he laughed.

Were I to task myself to tell exactly
How much her love has really meant to me
I'd botch it since I speak so matter-of-factly.
I'd need to fill two volumes, even three.
    Embarrassed, stilted speech could ne'er succeed.
    Best if I leave this poem for her to read.

Frank Sutton

NIGHTINGALE

There are so many people so cruel and unkind
What kind of damage have they done to mankind?
It's not Mother Nature or the world that is wrong
Or the God that we worship, to Him we belong.

It must be those people that govern and rule
That creates all wars, the earth to spoil
But in the end when we're all dead and gone
Nature takes over and the world carries on.

Let's stop this killing and give peace a chance
Love is the one thing we should try to enhance
For what is the point when mankind has gone
Dead men can't hear the nightingale's song.

Keith Onslow

CAT NAP

Pussycat, pussycat, sleeping on a wall,
Oh, be careful mind you do not fall,
Sleeping there so cosy, enjoying your dream
Of saucers of milk and lashings of cream,
Pussycat, pussycat, it's time for a walk,
Visit old Tom cat and have a talk,
He'll tell of his youth and how he met Kitty,
How he fell in love because she was pretty,
He'll remember the time he wandered away
And was missing as long as a month and a day,
Poor Kitty was pining and then to her cost,
She wandered away and also was lost.
And then one day to their owner's delight
He happened to see a wondrous sight,
A proud Tom and Kitty coming up the road,
And walking behind a sight to behold,
They had brought six little offspring back to the fold,
And it had all ended happily or so I was told.

M Wevill

LOVE WISH

Wishing words of colours
  trying to be free
Wanting to run riot
  dancing on thoughts
  holding on tight
Must be strong
  to be able to fight
  then it will explode in delight
  and time will tell its tale tonight.

Emily Hayes

MY HOME

You may travel the world
Seeing wonderful sights
Spend days in the sea
Enjoy warm sultry nights
But travelling home
As we pass fields of green
Nothing means more
Than our county to me
We have everything near
The rambling moors
Where sheep graze
And ponies are seen
Heather, gorse
The colours enchanting
With miles of green
The tors like small mountains
Are visibly seen
We enjoy all the best
That a country can hold
The sea surrounds, beaches
And history unfolds
We may have more rain
Than sun and blue skies
But that doesn't deter
People coming for miles
The warmth of the people
The breathtaking views
Devon will leave an impression on you

Jeanette Gaffney

THE SQUASHED ANT!

A squashed ant one day I saw
A squashed ant on the floor.
That poor little ant that didn't live
I wished a life to it I could give.
It eats sweet stuff, lots of it
This ant had muscles, he was fit!
I picked it up and shook it about
He was dead without a doubt
That poor ant that day I saw
I put it down onto the floor.

Samantha Sullivan (10)

TALKING OF LOVE NOT DECEIT

If he lied
Would the liar be true
If the words he spoke
Said I love only you
Yet deceit has no comparison
To a lover so bold
For you are his truth
When the truth is told

Warren Brown

LIFE AND LIVING

Life is for living so get on with your life
Life is for loving so forget all the strife,
Make every moment a spark of pleasure
Fight to make it more than a treasure

Life can be cruel when things go sour
Life's a bitter mistress so take a shower!
When you're refreshed and the water dries,
Wipe away the tears with a smile in your eyes

Life is an ocean you make for the shore,
Life gives you hope so you try once more,
Life's for the living but life never lasts
The very last chapter the great Amen blasts

The great Amen has sounded life and living are o'er,
You played your part, but lacked the art
Of living for evermore.

J Quick

I HAVE YOUR TEETH

I have your teeth
my daughters,
in oval
fine bone china pots.
The shoes you wore
before
you walked into the world.
Clothes,
so small,
wrapped within
the handmade shawl.
And,
as you grew
I spoke to you,
words that talked
in different ages.
But now,
I stand
engulfed in thoughts,
listening to
our distant strangeness.

Pamela Gardner

SUNSHINE

The sun was shining with all its might
Filling the earth with its dazzling light
Waking the flowers from their dark moist beds
Warming all their different coloured heads
Drying the butterflies' bright new wings
While all around hummed many flying things
Making the day feel oh so fine
That's what happens when we see the sun shine.

June M Peek

RIO DE JANEIRO - 1962

The bare foot burns on golden sand,
A red-hot sun on shoulders, back and legs.
A lazy walk to ocean blue - so cool,
First steps up to the knees, then bliss,
Sheer transports of delight.

With arms a-pressing ears quite tight
Into the heaving mass of ocean - I dive

Salt on lips, in eyes and ears
There can't be any other fears
Of leaving this drab world behind.
Way to go - a lovely way to go,
(Maybe the best)

The heaving waters, seen and known it all before,
Have room for generations, and more.
To taste the salt, and hear the gurgle in the ears
And know the time has come - to die.

And that's it - what more?

For those who think there's life hereafter
Please take a seat, and bear my laughter
The life we lead is one big con
That through the years goes on and on
And on, and on, and on.

R Sassi

TOWER BLOCKS TRANSFORMED

The moon sails between
twin towers stark against the sky
trailing misty veils of cloud.
The landing lights - ghost lit columns,
wan beacons in the chilly air.
All around is silence
broken by the distant barking of dogs
or sudden bursts of frenzied miaows -
a meeting of the local cats' club.
The moon is lost behind a rainy mist.
A solitary bird heralds the false dawn
soon to be joined by its fellows
in joyful chorus.
Then comes the hum of traffic
soft, then growing stronger.
The twin towers are transformed.
Stark no more against the violet sky.
Twinkling lights appear,
no longer are the windows blank,
the dwellers are stirring
preparing for the daily toil.
The twin towers are alive,
throbbing with life.

Ivy Allpress

VINTAGE MILITARY TRANSPORT

They come all clean and resplendent
To the vintage motor show
Each one has an interesting history
As they line up in a row

Military transport from the ages
With badge and battalion crest
Veterans of far off wars
They fought and passed the test

Deep down in chassis crease
Lay grains of sand, from deserts far
Or dust from some foreign road
Jeeps and tanks and armoured car

Men who into battle drove
Have gone, or grown old
Every single one a hero
Their stories almost forgotten, or untold

But these khaki tools of war
The remaining gallant few
Stand proudly in this English field
Old, but as good as new.

Keith Coleman

CREAKING KNEES

Many years have passed between us
adding wrinkles under our eyes,
each day has been different
now we're creaking our knees in time.
So long have we been together
I don't remember the years apart,
age has made no difference
to our together creaking hearts.

Now in our twilight years
our bodies begin to fade,
sharing together our memories
of a time in a different age.
Creaking our knees together
while walking hand in hand,
heading for a distant light
into a creaking land . . .

C Leith

THE KNOWING

I am a leaf in the wind,
And the wind takes me,
To be blown, alone and solitary
Left floating upon a pond.

I am the leaf,
Which flutters from a branch
Where children play amongst me
Unknowingly crush me into the soil that gave me.

And I am the autumn,
Full of beautiful golden death,
Buried deep in earth which bore me,
To await the time, when
I am spring.

Pam Hayhurst

THE BIG CAT

With muscled body, so black and lean
so quietly he suddenly appears
piercing eyes so clear and green
to stare and make our limbs to shake.

To us he shows no fear
he creeps with stealth
amongst the fields and woodland
or across the open moor.

This creature who stalks
by day and night
his unsuspecting prey to find
a sheep or perhaps a deer.

The experts say he is not here
this black cat
but we know, we've seen 'he is here'.

Lydia E Stanton

BOTTLED DREAMS

Many, many years ago;
I put a message in a bottle,
And it floated far out to sea
To date no one has answered it . . .
But perhaps one day . . . one day
One day . . . one day . . . maybe!

Many, many years ago;
I aspired to achieve a dream,
And my dream it lingers still,
To date I've not achieved it;
But perhaps one day . . . one day
One day . . . one day . . . one day . . .
One day . . . I will!

Clive Blake

WINTER NIGHT

The world is white tonight.
All day, so quietly,
Like soft white leaves
From a great white tree,
The snowflakes fluttered down
Upon the town.

The world is bright tonight.
Above the silent town
The silver moon
Is leaning down,
And on the streets so white
Pour silver light.

Jenny Hill

CLIMBING TOGETHER

Of a sudden I see this glint with chiaroscuro clouds
Wrestling
       Colossal
              Stark
The light in crevices breaking confusedly in your face
Squint
       Grimace
             Grin

Ralf Thorgood

TWIST YOUR NOSE

A lone trumpet in the company of strings,
Bold as brass with violins,
A joker amongst a flush of flowers,
Roses, lavender and delphinium towers.

Such a simple flower, so hard to resist,
No playful names like love in a mist,
A flaming flower that is truly alight,
Cheerful, dazzling and uniquely bright.

Parading his colours without any fear,
A jester, a prince, or a bold cavalier,
Invading the border with random excursions,
Or have I just simply been casting nasturtiums.

Malcolm Watson

MEMORY

Here I cry a tear for you,
A little white gem shows in a shaft of silver light,
Rolling down my cheek it falls,
A teardrop lost in the fire,
You stay in me as an eternal memory,
I'll let the world know you were mine,
But you belong to the heavens,
You belong to the night,
Give your soul to the people of darkness,
And make way for new life,
I could never forget you,
A burning desire remains in me still,
In my heart I will keep you my friend,
Let go of your soul,
And some day we will meet again.

Jonathan Wooddin (12)

WILD HORSE

Powerful horse with a long graceful stride,
With a coat of silk and deep, dark eyes.
With a flying tail and a flowing mane,
A horse un-used to bit or rein.
Gorgeous horse, wild and free,
How I wish you could belong to me.

Jo Bellamy (13)

THE WIND

The wind can be a tyrannical blast
Before which, all bow down
Even the oak, king of trees
Must bend his leafy crown.
But wind can also be a sigh
Like a child caressed by sleep
Gently stirring blades of grass
And the billows on the deep.

Brenda Benton

TEARS

I will try my hardest
to forget you, now I know
I will never have you
that will be the hardest
thing for me to do.

You will never see me shed a tear
that I will never do
in front of you

Tears will be pouring from my heart
instead of my eyes

Inside I feel like dying
but you will never see me crying.

Rachel Wake

RETIREMENT

At last your working days are over
And you believe you'll be in clover.
With stress and strain now in the past
You think you can relax at last.
Alas this dream will never be
As many others hold the key.
The phone rings and you're in demand
From those who need a helping hand.
Can you deliver meals on wheels
And aid the needy with many ills?
One day a week is all we ask
It really is an easy task.
Soon at everyone's beck and call
You end up saying yes to all.
You can't refuse the young and old
Who 'twixt them both will shape the mould.
With days so full from morn to night
The odd free hour is pure delight.
You have no job to hide behind
And begin to mourn the daily grind.
If you had known how it would be
Once you were footloose and fancy free
You'd have laid your plans a while before
And stayed at work for evermore!

Tessa Dewhurst

REJOICE

Long ago in Bethlehem
To the Virgin Mary was born a son
In a manger full of hay
Rejoice, rejoice hear what I say.

He came to save all mankind
For all the wrongs ever done
Hear his word and obey
Rejoice, rejoice hear what I say.

He healed the sick, loved the poor
The dear Lord Jesus was there for all
He is the truth, he is the way
Rejoice, rejoice hear what I say.

They crucified him on the cross
He died to save each one of us
He rose again, is alive today
Rejoice, rejoice hear what I say.

Jean H Davenport

GRANNIE'S DAY

Grannie, what was it like, without TV?
Getting a job without a CV?
Washing in a tub all made of brick?
Surely all this bother got on your wick.

Reading a book, with only a candle for light,
Doing the chores, way into the night,
Fetching the water from the village pump,
Spilling some, and getting a smack on the rump.

Walking a few miles to the local school,
Stopping to skate on the village pool,
Getting to school late, and getting detention,
On getting home, that you didn't mention.

You blamed getting home late on the lads down the street,
Especially the one with the big smelly feet.
You did your own sewing, and mending of socks,
You didn't worry about what's on the box.

Apples were plenty, when you went scrumping,
If you got caught, that meant a thumping.
It was your own fault, if your tummy was aching,
Some apples for you, and some were for baking.
You are all right, Grannie, the Lord is with you.
He is waiting for the day, when you're with him too.

Don Friar

THE TINY MIRACLE

From nothing, chaos, and blast,
It formed, perfect, invisible, small,
Vibrating in perfect unison,
To fill a cosmos vast, so fast,
Unexplained,
Created by God, related to all.

From the furthest star and everywhere,
The tiny atoms pervade,
They're the stars, moon and garden rose,
The mountain, sea, a luscious pear,
Inexplicable,
The smallness from nothing was made.

Does time reveal the pages
Of a history already ordained?
Is there a final chapter,
Beyond time's eternal rages?
Is the invisible, vibrating, unchanged,
For the future there to find?

Predictability magnifies the mystery,
Restores the wonder of life, of being,
A beginning, an end, linked by smallness,
Unchanging in cosmic history,
It fills the void miraculously,
This hydrogen atom, created from nothing.

The mushroom clouds, so swiftly climb,
Primeval power from an eternal source,
Fate's ultimate tragic twist,
A return to oblivion, an end to earth's time,
For what began as a mysterious gift,
Man may use for a cataclysmic force.

Iolo Lewis

WHAT AM I?

When you're seven months old you may have four,
As you grow older you get a few more.
By the time you're five you should have twenty,
At seven years old you are a bit empty.
What am I?

As time goes on you need some attention,
And everyone gives you a little mention.
You have to visit someone, who you hate,
Have something put in to stop the ache.
What am I?

When you're twelve you've got thirty-six,
Some are crumbling and need to be fixed.
You visit the man you still have fear,
Have some repairs before they disappear.
What am I?

When you are adult you may lose them all,
To eat your meals you look quite a fool.
Then the day comes when you get another pair,
You can take these out and give them lots of care.
I am teeth!

Eileen Denham

I WILL SEE THE WORLD

To feel the sun's warmth, to see a blue sky above.
To grasp tender hands, of the person your heart loves.
To see the flowers bloom, in a garden laid with care.
A heart that knows happiness, a world of love you share.

To see the birds above, while in the heavens, they fly.
To ease the pain of children, when you hear them cry.
To touch golden leaves, while on the trees they grow.
Feeling gentle flakes, falling from the sky as snow.

To hear a child's voice, but never seeing the face.
Visions in your mind, no words could ever erase.
To clasp a tiny hand, joy is yours, forever more.
A gentle breeze blows, a sandy beach, a golden shore.

Feeling the warmth of the sun, never seeing skies of blue.
Tender words are spoken, by the one I love so true.
Touching things that grow, bright pictures in my mind.
Seeing all God's creations, this I cannot, for I am blind.

Things I cannot see, pictures of all, are given by you.
Loving words you have said, I know your love is true.
I will see the world, God created, if I reach heaven.
No more will I be blind, a new sight, I'll be given.

Kevin P S Collins

STEVIE

My first granddaughter so sweet and small
Arrived this sunny Monday to the joy of us all
A beautiful little girl, dark hair, tiny hands, tiny feet
Born to my beloved daughter Lyn and son-in-law Robert
To make their life complete
With countenance more pretty than a spring morn
Dear little Stevie Elizabeth Rianna
Grandma loves you and thanks God you were born

Patricia Summerfield

OUTRAGEOUS CAT

My cat is special, he is rare,
Loves to watch me brush my hair.
He is glossy - loves eating fish,
Especially when it's from *my* dish.
Drinks the water from my glass,
Doesn't even stop to ask.
When he hears the ringing tone,
Comes to purr upon the phone.
Start my work - I mop the floor,
Jet, runs in with muddy paws.
Make the bed - all nice and neat,
He jumps in and out of the sheets.
Do the ironing, oh my Lord!
Up he leaps upon the board.
Rest in the chair for just a minute,
I get up - he is in it!
Just when I think he is rather sweet,
He drops a mouse right at my feet.
I take a bath - alone I think,
Jet spies on me - sits in the sink.
If that's not enough for you,
He even follows me in the loo!
It's time for bed, it's plain to see,
How do I know? He's telling me.
Outrageous cat - divine feline,
'Come along then, sleeping time.'

Jillian Hockley

LIFE

Roses in my head, violets in my voice
Would I stay here if I had a choice?
Pictures on the wall, telling of the past
Faces in the mirror, time is fading fast.
Bottles on the wall, kids are playing around
Wishing I was young again so I wouldn't feel so down
Searching through the emptiness of my sunken heart
Looking for a reason for why we had to part.
To all my questions why, the answer I don't know
The empty shell I'm living does not know where to go.
To turn to someone in times of trouble
When all around are bricks and rubble
Fallen from the place I'm living
Time to accept the life I've been given.

Now that I'm dying, how long will it be
For the ones that I love to forget about me?
Will it be days, months or years
Or hours to dry those crocodile tears.
When you said you loved me were you being sincere
Or is it your guilty conscience you fear?
The sands of time are running out
It makes me think; what was life all about?
And now I've finally come to the end
To the one I love this message I send;
Ashes to ashes, dust to dust
Was I in love or was I in lust?

Alan Colvill

ODE TO A TELEPHONE

Where would I be without you
Tell me what I would do
I love ev'rything about you
I know you love me too

To some you're just an object
A means as to an end
But you'll never be a reject
While I've got time to spend

I'll talk to and caress you
Your receiver I will warm
I always will protect you
And keep you from all harm

I love to hold you tightly
Whisper sweet things in your ear
I use you day and nightly
I'll always love you do not fear

And if you're feeling lonely
Just give a little ring
And I'll speak to you only
You precious little thing

When you ring I'll be there
I'll answer straight away
My soul to you I will bare
You get me through each day.

Mary Trench

BLINDED BY THE ECLIPSE

Grey sighs of the sun
Bathe a busy world to quietness.
Feathers roost on a quick night;
Their false dawn
Fades into light . . .
Time spent watching
Like a daydream,
Slowed the eyes
To *real* darkness.

Donald James Munday

Passing Time

Through high wind and pouring rain
Watch the journey of the train.
The carriages as they rock and sway -
Carry the people at the end of day.

Through barrier down, that makes a bar
To you sitting in your motorcar;
And as it passes you can dream
Of burning coals and hissing steam.

As it travels by so fast
Conjuring up pictures of days past;
But today's picture on Artist's easel
Is not of steam but modern diesel.

So onward to its destination
End of line - terminus station.

Next when at 'flashing lights' you wait
That once was level crossing gate -
You can watch the passing train
Travelling through high wind and rain.

Rod Gill

THE HANDY MAN

He starts a job with good intentions
But always gets the wrong dimensions
Yes dear, he says, I'll build that shed
And stands there scratching his bald head.
Now where's that nail, I had it here
I think it's time I had a beer
Meaning well he always does
And starts off with an energetic buzz
But I know in my heart
Although he makes a willing start
The end product I'll never see
Now he sits beneath the tree
Cooling off and building strength
To hammer in the next wood length
Gets up once more to start again
Now he says it looks like rain
I think I'll leave it just for now
And then he makes the same old vow
Tomorrow is another day
Now I'll put the tools away
That shed I fear is doomed to be
A mirage for eternity.

W Tutte

JUST ME!

Oh how wonderful it would be
Just to be pure and simply me!
But no! I have to be polite
And sweetly smile when all the while
I'm slowly seething up inside!
I must not rant or rage about
Or stamp my feet or even shout!
I must be circumspect and good
And do the things I really should.
Oh I must never break the law
Or listen at an open door.
I mustn't leave the washing up
Or dunk my biscuit in the cup.
I mustn't show how much I care,
Or take my clothes off anywhere.
That surely is not ever done,
But wouldn't it be lots of fun!
Why must I always have to take
The very smallest slice of cake?
Why can't I simply just be me
And take the largest piece I see!
Why must I never jump a queue
Or do the things I long to do?
Why must I be so meek and mild
When all I long to be is wild!
I must not be the first to leave
Or show my tears whene'er I grieve
But all the while just bravely smile.
Why can I never be
Just pure and simply me!

J D Winchester

RESURGAM

(A meditation for Easter, Millennium year)

Into the dark and dreaming days of winter
A restless urge, which may not be ignored,
Arises when the sun brings hope and warming.
Then Nature slowly shows the first response
By clothing Earth with colour and with fragrance -
A backcloth for the graciousness of life.

How fitting it was Spring which saw the Rising
After the three-day resting in the Tomb.
To Man, asleep, there also comes a summons;
He, too, must wake and work to make his earth
A place where peace and beauty shape together
A loving welcome for the Risen Lord.

Vivienne Constantinides

SCHOOL TRANSPORT - 1950s STYLE

We all stood waiting at the cross-roads,
Expressing irritation in our different ways.
To kill time, Barbara took out the mitten she was knitting,
And Lily softly crooned the latest smoochy tune, 'Dying for you'
(She was into Radio Luxembourg and weekend hops).
Joan morosely challenged the empty road
To roll a vehicle down its skittle run
And hoped it would be ours. 'The taxi's late *again*!'
She groaned. We all, like robots, checked our cheap wristwatches
And shook our heads and stamped, like carthorses
Impatient to be off. David, tongue out, notebook bent back
Cruelly, stabbed accents over his French prep,
Comparing, crossing out, and filling gaps from Jim's neat work.
Poor Jim, more than his life was worth to hide his book
Well-strapped inside his bag - a punch-up would ensue.
I watched them all and wished that I were dead.

A lorry rumbled past, and then a motorbike, two cars,
A van, which partly hid from view a stately, gliding ghost,
Sleek and slow. 'It is, it isn't! What the devil's that?' cried Jim
As it quietly drew up. Black Jack, familiar in his uniform,
Squeezed beetle brows into a gloomy frown.
'Watch it, you lot. The taxis are on hire;
We shouldn't use the hearse for the school run. I put two seats in,
Three in each row, and try to sit dead still. Don't mark the trim.'
Rigid with awe, like upright frozen corpses, we progressed
To the graveyard of our freedom.

S G Herbert

SEPTEMBER SUNSHINE

Birds in flight,
Muted summer sun.
Green pastures turning gold,
Young lambs released from the fold.

Projects nearly finished,
Back to school, complete another year.
Passed the Os,
The As? Would they be so clear.

The elderly, still very strong,
In heart and mind.
Quietly walk the hills,
Much peace to find.

Warmth of friendship,
Keeps us on our mettle.
Time for home,
Put on the kettle.

Rosemary J Povey

THEATRE

Weeks of seemingly endless rehearsals
Hours spent painstakingly learning lines
Shakespearean scenes of love, hate, fear and revenge;
Reflecting my own life, or how I wish it to be

As the opening night draws nearer,
Tensions are taken to unbearable heights
Patience and tolerance are forgotten words
Nicotine is worth its weight in gold

Final touches are made to costumes and set
Box office phones ring with last minute bookings
A once lively cast are now weary and tense
Everything seems destined to fail

The day arrives bringing nerves and excitement
As actors hurriedly get into costumes
Expectation takes its seat in the audience
The curtain rises and a miracle performs

Susannah Payne

TEARS FALL ABOVE ME LIKE RAIN

The orange glow of the fire filled all but the corners of the still room,
The red patterned carpet hides the additional paints falling from
$\qquad$ the young artist's hand.

The preserved dolphin swam through the cobwebs of time,
The sticky threads enveloping all that moved within,
Its wrath had ended, as now nothing moved.
The girl lay heaped, like a frightened mannequin,
Her body bent, cowering like a frightened puppy,
The echoes of footsteps had faded with her memory,
Her peace could not be reached until she was freed from her
$\qquad$ webbed cocoon.

A breeze shifted the air, new echoes carried, muffled by an
$\qquad$ ageing carpet,
Now tears fall above me like rain.

Emma Kirke

THE DAY HOSPITAL

An oasis of calm
In a world of strife
A chance to relax
And change your life.

How do we thank those
Who are busy and kind
Helping us cope
And find peace of mind.

I hope this will show you
In some small way
All the things
That we want to say.

D Creasey

HOMECOMING

Worn out and hungry I swallowed my pride
and headed for home - well no, for food,
for clothes instead of rags, sandals for bleeding feet,
and in return I'd work, nothing would be too menial.
Anything must be better than this - this degradation,
this wretched emptiness and nothing left to lose.
I nearly didn't make it; the way was long and hard,
it didn't seem like that the day I left,
my pocket full of money and my head full of dreams.

Too tired to raise my head I trudged and stumbled on,
dust in my eyes, sweat streaming down my back.
I didn't see him coming - the old man -
but he was running
with arms outstretched to greet me,
tears coursing down his cheeks.

I staggered then and fell. Down on my knees
I tried to say my piece; he wouldn't listen.
Breathless from his exertion, he stooped
and put his arms around me,
held me to his chest - his breast.
I, ready for the tomb had found a womb.
And suddenly I wept; suddenly I knew
it wasn't food I craved, though I was starving.
It was love. And when he said 'My boy!
So glad to have you back. We thought you'd died,'
I just broke down and cried.

Helene McLeod

My Dream

In my dream I walk alone
on an empty and deserted road,
as I walk through
dust and dirt
I see a small and dark code.

On the code are letters
representing a land,
I didn't know this at first
I was standing on quick-sand.

I held my breath
and down I went,
leaving behind the deserted land
when I realised
this is no ordinary sand.

Fish, mermaids, dolphins too
I was looking at
an ocean covered with blue,
I swam to a mermaid
and asked her where I was,
all she said was
follow the buzz.

After a while a siren was heard
every creature
turned into a bird,
they flowed away from this ocean
and landed on an island named Potion.

One of the birds picked me up
threw me in a black hole of cream
and that was the end
of my not so wonderful dream.

Sonya Nikolosina (11)

FIONA AND ANDREW - WEDDED BLISS

Greetings from us both upon this your wedding day
And some helpful hints for Andrew to help him on his way

Since now that you have said 'I do' and Fiona is your wife
There are certain things you need to know, to ensure a quiet life

Over 30 years ago, Fiona made a master plan
To lead a life of leisure, and to find the perfect man

Her task would not be easy since high standards they were set
But she would only marry when the ideal man was met

She needed him to cook, she needed him to dust
She needed him to sew, and ironing was a must

He would take the rubbish out, rid the garden of its weeds
Wash the car on Sundays, and satisfy her needs

In fact what Fiona really needed to ensure a blissful life
Was not so much a husband but an understanding wife!

She scoured the land for many years and thought that she was beat
Until one drunken evening, it was Andrew she did meet

So unbeknown to him, she put him to the test
And whilst he wasn't perfect, he was better than the rest!

He was charming, he was witty, he was handsome, he was kind
And whatever tasks she set him he didn't seem to mind

He was the ultimate in chivalry, a rare and dying breed
He was the ideal husband, she was happy to concede

So congratulations Andrew upon your wedding day
There's nothing more for you to fear, it's downhill all the way

Now please forgive us for our humour because our words are
                                                said in jest
Since undoubtedly in Fiona, you have found the very best

She is the rose amongst the thorns, the diamond glint on snow
A very special friend, who's a privilege to know

So now that you have made your vows and the journey had begun
We wish you every happiness as you venture forth as one

Lesley Scott

THE COCKNEY SPARROWS

Where have all the sparrows gone?
I would like to know
They were always with us
In sunshine, rain and snow
Have they gone to the country
Away from the noisy streets
Where cattle graze peacefully
And a new born lamb bleats?
They were not birds of paradise
Their plumage a browny grey
Neither were they songsters
They just chirped all the day
If you should chance to see them
Please let me know
Come back cockney sparrows
Because we love you so
Have they gone to another place
Where the sun shines all the day
In a field of daffodils
Where little children play?
Beside a gentle river
Where crystal waters flow
Come back cockney sparrows
Because we love you so.

R H Baillie

SLEEPING BEAUTY

Untouched by time's extortionate demands
Like a recumbent rose slowly in bloom
My love obeys slumber's princely commands
Likening high tower to lowly tomb
Her breast an altar on which I'd worship
I'd sleep myself and dream a life with her
But address the achievement of her crypt
For by her loss the world's a widower
To seek, to dare, to pierce through the bower
And slumber's clinging affections dismiss
Ransoming her from the shrouds of the tower
Gracing lips as red as a blush with a kiss
   I should not venture for fear of the fall
   But would rather die than try not at all

John Dickie

RAPE BY MASCULINITY

Who is being raped? The woman
Who is she? A housewife or a prostitute
  a mother or a daughter
  a grandmother or a granddaughter
Who is the rapist? The man?
  No, but masculinity!
Why she? Why not he?
  She is weak, she is the victim;
  he is strong, he is the abuser
She loses her personal power
  her body has been raped
  her mind has been humiliated
  her spirit has gone, hidden
Whether being raped
  by close male acquaintances or strangers
  it hurts, the scars last forever!
She loses confidence on intimacy
  she loses herself
  and even her soul
His anger has shown
  by his hatred and fear towards women
  he wants to control and dominate
  either by raping women or men.
Is he a real man? *No!*
What is behind rape?
  Violence!
Rape is inhumane
  her humanity has been violated
  her womanhood has been degraded
How can she get healing and gain back her power?

Mei Yuk Wong

MY SISTER

I look up to you in many ways,
for how you still smile, on unhappy days.
Sometimes I wonder, just how you cope,
because you never give in or sit and mope.

You have lots of courage, I admire in you.
Whatever the trouble, you see it through.
Your inner strength, your courage and love,
was born in you from the angels above.

You deserve so much, for being you,
for the sacrifices you've made, and all that you do.
If words could make your life the best,
this poem wouldn't end, the pen wouldn't rest.

I wish for you, good luck, good health,
I wish the stars to bring you wealth.
Though there is one star, that shines so bright,
it will always be your guiding light.

You and I grew up together
And will always be friends, for ever and ever.

Susan Serjeant

THE WAITING ROOM

There I sat, in the waiting room,
Reading a magazine, two weeks old
Some people had colds, others talked of doom
On the walls, were pictures, surrounded with gold,
The floor was carpeted, but very worn
Children, played, with second hand toys
And, a pregnant lady was there, to check her first born
She was asked, if she preferred girls, or boys
A young girl called out the patients' names,
Then they would disappear behind the blue door
While waiting, the wallpaper presented games,
How many times I counted the squares, I'm not sure
Here in this room, diseases abound, too many
When I see the doctor, will I be full of flu,
Or pass on a virus to others, it's uncanny
One thing's for sure, I'm feeling low too
I wouldn't mind, but I only need an injection,
So I can go on holiday, in the east
When the doctor sees me, his only intention,
Will be, to get rid of me, at the least.

T G Bicknell

FAREWELL TO SUMMER

The falling leaves from browning trees
Herald the approach of a winter freeze.
The lowering evening sun, its reddening orb alight,
Dips slowly below the horizon each lengthening night.
At dawn we may see a coat of frost
Has covered our growing garden compost.
Autumn stirs!

A Jessop

THAT CAT

He lives next door
That furry thing
He wags his tail
His bell does ring

He purrs all day
All night too
Just lies about
With nothing to do

When I see him
He's often asleep
And if he's not
To the birds he creeps

I wish that I
Could be like that
Just lazing about
Just like that cat.

J Roberts

THE OLDER DOG

'Oh! I know that I'm grey and a bit grizzled, too,
But it doesn't diminish my love - for you.
We've been through puppyhood and middle-aged spread,
And it's true - these days - I do like my bed . . .
But fetch me my lead and pick up your keys,
And I'll race you a mile! (In dignified ease.)'

Joyce Dobson

IT'S NOT EASY TO BE A CHRISTIAN

It's not easy to be a Christian
When, arising in the morning,
Everything seems to go all wrong,
Of course it's not so easy then
To smile, and sing a happy song

It's not easy to be a Christian
When everything does not go,
The way you've already planned.
When your friends and loved ones
Cannot really understand.

It's not easy to be a Christian
When you think that you've only done
Just what for them is truly right,
Then of course they do not agree
And really get so uptight.

It's not easy to be a Christian
When you find out that your new friends
Do always talk behind your back,
Or when your husband comes home
With the news that he's got the sack.

It's not easy to be a Christian
When you've put all your washing out,
Then the rain comes down in torrents,
Soaking everything through and through,
For your neighbour forgot to shout.

It's not easy to be a Christian
When it's put out another day,
And it's all but nearly dry,
Down it goes, as the clothes line breaks,
Oh, then you could really cry.

But it's easier to be a Christian
When we commune with God in prayer,
Whatever the trial or problem,
We can feel He's always there.

Yes it's easier to be a Christian
When we just let Him guide our day,
Then following in His footsteps
We can always be sure to say,

'Lord help me to be a Christian
For things are not going my way.
The road is dark and difficult,
So hear me Lord as I pray.'

Oh Lord I want to be a Christian
Telling out Your message of love,
Lord help me to be a Christian
'Til we meet in Heaven above.

E C Squire

LIFE

(Dedicated to the memory of Ernest John Butler and Edwin Brian Taylor)

The world is always harder
If you think and see

The world is forever turning
That's how life is for me

So if you're hurt and crying
Feel the cool breeze

Think of all the good things
And think of me

Alice Sanders (7)

TO JANE

Do you recall that autumn night,
When I turned and saw you in that golden light?
Your oval face, a warming smile;
I was bewitched! Am still awhile.
That voice, so deep and strong and soft,
Must hail from Heaven, God's highland croft.
And what hair! And what eyes!
For one so young, and one so wise.
I know love well and you are she;
Now all that matters: what say you me?

JSC Sutherland

IDLE THOUGHTS

It really is strange how the mind just wanders.
Why did I think of the Thames just then,
The Moira River and the House of Wonders,
The watch I once won or my bright red pen?

The stuff that dreams are made of do vary.
Erotic or chaste, ridiculous or sublime,
A day on the beach or that glass of chilled sherry,
Sketches in a cerebral collage of images divine.

Have you ever imagined yourself as that seaman of old,
The conqueror of Everest or a soldier of fortune?
Have you never stuck out your chest to win a medal of gold,
Or kicked at that ball to score a goal most opportune?

What then are my sketch thoughts most treasured?
My wedding day, of course, and that last meal with my parents.
A walk atop Masada and my first sight of a leopard,
And a Christmas yet to come with me loaded with presents!

Francis de Lima

PROGRESS

Modern ways are strange indeed,
Given to believe, this is exactly what we need!

Resting on a bench one day, I quickly was aware
That the chap seated beside me was talking to thin air!
I think I'll move away I quietly said to self
So inch by inch a-edging and with a certain stealth
I quit my place and started off
Adding a self-effacing cough.

Just as I passed this crazy fellow
He gave a laugh and then a bellow.
I threw him a glance, covert I'll own,
What did I see, he was on the phone!
Clamped to his right ear and almost unseen
Was this minuscule gadget, you know what I mean!

Come to think of it, now, in bus or in street
Mobiles start buzzing, for job or to greet,
Strap hanging on the tube like sardines in a tin,
What we hear nowadays is ring, ring a ring-ring.
If one is not so lucky it could indeed be near
Squashed up against another, dinging in the ear.

So many things today one's urgently urged to do,
Shop by post, fax someone, plastic cards use too.

Was in this shop and queuing, anxious to get out,
Had in hand a loaf of bread and a couple of trout,
The person just before me, for a siege had bought,
Couldn't pay with money, was the cards she sought,
Out came a sheaf, unsure what she was about,
I always seem to end up thus, it makes me want to shout.

The pace of life increases, where, will it all end?
Sitting on a cloud I expect, mobiling to a friend!

Daphne McFadyen

PUZZLED?

I'm puzzled about puzzles, anagrams and Mensa games
The crosswords which have numbers instead of usual names
They're like a drug, they get to me and I sit up half the night
Trying hard to get the answers, I really have to get them right
There's a row of numbers, you must find the next one in the line
I've tried so hard to work it out, I think it's number nine
But then, I'm not so sure, I'll have to do it all again
And so I write the numbers down it's doing in my brain.
At last I get the answer, I think, thank goodness that is done
I turn the page over and staring at me is another one
Now this one is quite different, there's six boxes printed here
One is not the same as the other five appear.
They've got numbers printed on them. A to F on back and front
The front ones you can see, for the back you have to hunt.
I try to turn the paper round to see the other side
Oh! Silly me I really should not have even tried
Now I've found a puzzle, this one looks easier to do
I've got to spot the difference, first one, the baby's got no shoe
Another one, Mum's got no hat, Dad's coat is black, the cat is white
The bird is missing, the door is shut, there's an extra plate, Tom's got
no kite
Good there's only two to go then I feel I can relax
The mat is round and Phillip's trumpet appears to be a sax
Now that's the lot, I must give up, then I spot another book
I'll open up the pages and just take a little look.
There's a puzzle that I'm sure won't take me very long to do.
It looks quite easy, let me see, I must find out who is who
Well B will match the figure two and D with number three
If I add two cabbages, four turnips and a pea
Will I get a horse with a multi-coloured mane?
Oh lock me up, these puzzles have driven me insane

Gladys Baillie

WHITE CITY TIMES (AN EXTRACT)

Nightmare tabloid vampires
terrorised this quaking child,
trapped 'twixt sea-green
hallway walls so tall -
Garth was no saviour seen.

Walls that would reveal
intrusive lightning.
Quick! Cover the mirrors,
secrete the stainless steel
and any shining tile,
lest it catch the wicked smile
of cunning thunder.

Toilet time ordeal -
wiping his skinny bum
with torn pages
of the Daily Drum,
its lurid headlines smugly
smeared on shivering white cheeks -
its most discriminating
readership for weeks.

In Melbourne Park he
threw balls to shoulder -
shaking heights,
as if to pierce the bolder
clouds, then vainly tried to
catch them as they fell
like giant meteors in flight . . .

Wes Ashwell

DARK THOUGHTS

The snakes unravel
Yellow and black
Their menacing movement
Disturbs peace

The cords entwine
Red and purple
Their anger ripples
Disturbs peace

The elastic snaps
Grey and broken
Opens a vault
Disturbs peace

Inside the vault
Black and blue
A serene statue
Makes peace

Salvages the wreckage
A golden glimmer
Warm and calm
Inner peace

Miriam Eissa

JUST WHY WAS I BORN

In the silence of my room
I laid upon my bed
And let my idle thoughts
Roam around inside my head
When suddenly my thoughts began to form
And question after question came
Like 'Just why was I born?
What is the purpose of my life?
Do people hold me dear?
And would they really miss me
If I were not here?'
Then the questions began to change
To thoughts of every kind
'Why was there so much sickness
In body and in mind?
Why do the cries for help so often go unheard?'
Surely we would succour
A fallen little bird
'Are we too busy to pay a little heed
And lend a helping hand
To those who are in need?'
So in the silence of my room
I began to see the light
Perhaps the purpose of my life
Is to give help where I might
To bring a little cheer to those
Whose life is far from bright
So if I can lend a helping hand
In any shape or form
I might find this is the reason
Just why I was born.

Ruby A Okker